Enhancing Leadership Effectiveness Through Psychological Type

A DEVELOPMENT GUIDE FOR USING PSYCHOLOGICAL TYPE WITH EXECUTIVES, MANAGERS, SUPERVISORS, AND TEAM LEADERS

by Roger R. Pearman, Ed.D.

D1604526

CENTER FOR APPLICATIONS OF PSYCHOLOGICAL TYPE, INC.
GAINESVILLE, FLORIDA

Published by the Center for Applications of Psychological Type, Inc.
2815 NW 13th Street
Suite 401
Gainesville, Florida

ISBN 0-935652-48-5

Library of Congress Cataloging-in-Publication Data

Pearman, Roger R., 1956–
     Enhancing leadership effectiveness through psychological type:
a development guide for using psychological type with
executives, managers, supervisors, and team leaders/
by Roger R. Pearman

          p. cm.
Includes bibliographical references.
     ISBN 0-935652-45-0
     1. Leadership--Psychological aspects. 2. Typology (Psychology)
I. Title
BF637.L4P42 1999
158'.4--dc21

                              99-29112
                              COP

Contents

Introduction

Leaders for the next millennium understand that leadership requires *enhancing relationships* and *promoting creativity* among members of an organization. Relationships grow when understanding between individuals is established and when communicating effectively is a priority among members of the organization. Creativity is promoted when individuals feel included and integral to the future of the organization. This guide will help leaders understand their own leadership psychology and provide insights into the needs of those around them who are essential to fulfilling the organizational goals. With these insights, enhanced relationships and increased creativity can be achieved.

To underscore the importance of enriching our relationships in organizations, a careful study of the research and writings on leadership reveals several key reasons for leader effectiveness and ineffectiveness. Success and failure are primarily tied to developing constructive relationships among members of the team or organization, appropriate communications between leader and team members, and a demonstrated valuing of human differences. The table below summarizes leadership performance issues from three decades of research:[1]

Behavior Cluster	Percent Related To Success	Percent Related To Derailment*
Relationship Building *Caring, showing interest, fairness, and demonstrating trustworthiness and understanding*	23.8%	45.3%
Cognitive Complexity *Managing ambiguity, creativity, managing diversity and system complexity*	23.8%	10.5%
Communication *Supportive, informing, confronting, presentations, writing*	16.4%	5.2%
Self Management *Career ambition, courage, perseverance, self awareness, time management*	16.4%	26.3%
Decisiveness *Action orientation, command skills, organizing, prioritizing, results orientation*	13.4%	2%
Technical Ability *Functional skills, specific business*	5.9%	10.5%

* Due to failure to demonstrate behaviors in the cluster

Introduction

Fortunately for us, the model of psychological type on which this guide is based provides a comprehensive format for addressing and developing leadership effectiveness in those areas identified above as most critical to leadership. Psychological type assumes that relationships can be enhanced when differences are understood and valued. Of importance for leaders, type reveals that learning to access and appropriately express different mental competencies is crucial to building relationships, communicating appropriately, and promoting synergy among members of a team. This guide will be useful for executives, managers, and supervisors who wish to:

- increase their effectiveness at motivating others,
- improve productivity and job satisfaction, and
- improve their awareness of their personal leadership style and of self-imposed barriers to development.

How will this guide help you enhance your leadership effectiveness?

The first step to enhancing effectiveness is becoming more aware of your behavior and how your personal psychology influences that behavior. Research on how leaders learn and change shows that those who are self-monitoring and open to feedback grow quickly and get the most out of learning opportunities.[2] Therefore, looking through this guide and gaining clarity about your own style is an important first step. As indicated above, so much depends on behaviors for relationship building and interpersonal style that this guide is primarily focused on these aspects of leadership. There is an explicit link between type and leadership behaviors throughout this guide. Consequently, *by gaining clarity about your own type, you can have a deeper awareness of your leadership strengths and potential developmental needs.*

A second step is to list ways that you use *all aspects* of type as part of your everyday behavior. You are encouraged to read all sixteen descriptions and <u>underline</u> all those behaviors that you recognize as part of your behavioral repertoire. This will confirm the extensive range of type-related behaviors you comfortably express. Then reread the descriptions and *[bracket]* any behavior that *you know you should express to increase your effectiveness.* In this way, you can identify a pattern of behaviors that you need to add to your range of responses.

Finally, while you may not—nor need to—know the types of those around you, you can see that various responses are needed to address different types. In other words, knowing about a range of responses and ways of sharing information increases the chances that you will try several ways to communicate information. Clarity about our own style makes it easier to know the baseline and adjust as the situation requires.

Introduction

What is the "lesson" from psychological type needed to enhance leadership?

Psychological type enables you to identify both basic interpersonal qualities and a fluid use of mental functions. Psychological type is a model for understanding patterns in perceiving information and making decisions.[3] As simple as this sounds, type assumes the use of eight mental capacities and competencies in various powerful ways. Four of these capacities are related to perceiving information *(known as Introverted Sensing, Introverted Intuition, Extraverted Sensing, and Extraverted Intuition)* and four are connected to decisiveness about the information we have gathered *(known as Introverted Thinking, Extraverted Thinking, Introverted Feeling, and Extraverted Feeling)*. These capacities will be explored in more depth below.

Type is also a model for explaining the habits of mind each person uses for adjusting and responding to everyday demands using our perceiving and judging functions. Because these habits of mind promote typical behavioral expressions, psychological type also gives us a handle on the differences in the work and interpersonal styles we see around us in organizations, at home, and in our communities.

To help you develop an initial understanding of psychological type, key assumptions are outlined below. An additional link to leadership behavior is provided.

Working Assumptions

- There are alternating cycles of mental energy which each of us uses. Extraversion is attending to the people, places, and events outside of our skin and Introversion is attending to the thoughts, ideas, and feelings we have inside our skin. Leaders need to attend to the situations around them (by extraverting) and their insights about these situations (by introverting).
- There are two general ways each of us attends to information: through our sensing of the details, and through our intuiting of patterns. Both are innate and essential to the leadership processes of awareness, and identification of facts and meanings.
- There are two general ways of making decisions: through analyzing the cause and effect logic of a situation, and through understanding the values and interpersonal consequences of a situation. Deciding by Thinking (analytical criteria) or Feeling (value related criteria) about situations are critical capacities for getting the job done.
- There is a primary use of sensing, intuiting, thinking, or feeling in either an extraverted or introverted way. Further, both attitudes of

Introduction

extraverting and introverting are actively used in balancing perceiving and judging information.

- Although all dimensions of type are available to each person, individuals develop a pattern of perception and judgment to manage the events, tasks, and processes of leadership.

- Type development means that we are clear about our own type pattern, as well as how to utilize those dimensions that we do not access regularly. This underscores the aspect of effective leadership which demonstrates knowing what response is appropriate to the occasion.

- All dimensions of type are essentially valuable and constructive; however, they are not always effective when expressed in every situation. Awareness of our own typical responses and of those behaviors available to us as suggested by type theory tends to promote good leadership.

How is the model dynamic?

C.G. Jung and I.B. Myers wrote that type is about the active use of mental processes in our extraverting and introverting modes that we use in managing life. This requires a dynamic responsiveness and adaptation to the environment. Type helps us explore our patterns of responsiveness and adaptation. The initial step in understanding the dynamic is to realize that the mental processes outlined above are best seen in the illustration below.[4] Each individual uses all processes for daily activities but in a different sequence and with different amounts of psychological energy.

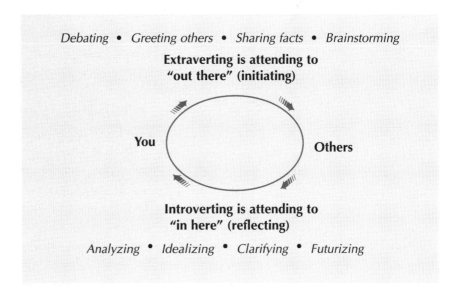

In our extraverting and introverting we use these mental capacities every day. Illustrations are provided in *italics* in the image above. In the space

Introduction

provided below, write down illustrations of your most recent awareness of each mental process:

Internal Perceiving

Introverted Sensing
(Clarifying–mental rehearsal)

_____

Introverted Intuiting
(Futurizing—imagining potential actions)

Internal Deciding

Introverted Thinking
(Analyzing—critiquing options)

_____

Introverted Feeling
(Idealizing–internal comfort, acceptance)

External Perceiving

Extraverted Sensing
(Quick identification of facts)

_____

Extraverted Intuiting
(Fluent discussion of patterns, ideas)

External Deciding

Extraverted Thinking
(External debate, pros/cons)

_____

Extraverted Feeling
(Expressed empathy, acceptance)

These functions can be easily seen in everyday behaviors of leaders. Appendix A provides a comprehensive list of leadership behaviors as related to mental functions. For a general understanding, consider the following behaviors that many managers have identified as expressions of their mental functions:

Behavior	Mental Function
• List all the key ideas about the topic	T_I Introverted Thinking
• Share some ideas with others about the presentation	N_E Extraverted Intuiting
• Create a group for brainstorming ideas	N_E Extraverted Intuiting
• Research the internet for new material on the topic	T_I Introverted Thinking
• Write out an outline with illustrations	S_I Introverted Sensing
• Do a mock presentation with some friends	T_E Extraverted Thinking
• Warmly greet people as they enter the room	F_E Extraverted Feeling
• Express various linkages during a presentation	N_E Extraverted Intuiting
• Use a logical "argument"	T_E Extraverted Thinking
• Use lots of facts, figures in talk	S_E Extraverted Sensing
• Mingle after the presentation	F_E Extraverted Feeling
• Write personal observations	S_I Introverted Sensing
• Prepare a presentation critique	T_I Introverted Thinking
• Call some participants, get feedback	T_E Extraverted Thinking
• Visualization, mental rehearsal	S_I Introverted Sensing

Introduction

Whole Type: Dynamics as Habits of Mind

You have the basics—extraverting, introverting, sensing, intuiting, thinking, feeling—and now you have examined the mental capacities or functions labeled Extraverted Feeling, Extraverted Thinking, Introverted Sensing, etc. As you can see, these mental functions are the integration of our extraverting and introverting processes with various ways of perceiving and deciding about our experience. It is precisely this balance between our introverting and extraverting processes which makes the type dynamic. The dynamic is based on the proposition that within each type is a preferred and primary mental function which is most evident and about which you (and others) are most aware. This primary mental process is aided and supported by a secondary, auxiliary process. And as indicated above, one of these is an extraverted process while the other is an introverted process. These processes provide a natural balance between extraverting and introverting, and perception and judgment, that enables us to successfully manage our life.

All of the descriptors in this guide are focused on the expressions of behaviors as evidence of this dynamic of the type. Note that if you do not know your four-letter type as sorted by the MBTI®, a self-sort guide is provided in Appendix B. As shorthand, the following table gives you the primary (dominant) and supporting (auxiliary) function for each type:

Type Code	Mental Functions/ Processes	
	Leading or Dominant	Supporting or Auxiliary
ISTJ — *Introverted Sensing w/ Extraverted Thinking*	S_I	T_E
ISFJ — *Introverted Sensing w/ Extraverted Feeling*	S_I	F_E
INFJ — *Introverted Intuition w/ Extraverted Feeling*	N_I	F_E
INTJ — *Introverted Intuition w/ Extraverted Thinking*	N_I	T_E
ISTP — *Introverted Thinking w/ Extraverted Sensing*	T_I	S_E
ISFP — *Introverted Feeling w/ Extraverted Sensing*	F_I	S_E
INFP — *Introverted Feeling w/ Extraverted Intuition*	F_I	N_E
INTP — *Introverted Thinking w/ Extraverted Intuition*	T_I	N_E
ESTP — *Extraverted Sensing w/Introverted Thinking*	S_E	T_I
ESFP — *Extraverted Sensing w/Introverted Feeling*	S_E	F_I
ENFP — *Extraverted Intuition w/Introverted Feeling*	N_E	F_I
ENTP — *Extraverted Intuition w/Introverted Thinking*	N_E	T_I
ESTJ — *Extraverted Thinking w/Introverted Sensing*	T_E	S_I
ESFJ — *Extraverted Feeling w/Introverted Sensing*	F_E	S_I
ENFJ — *Extraverted Feeling w/Introverted Intuition*	F_E	N_I
ENTJ — *Extraverted Thinking w/Introverted Intuition*	T_E	N_I

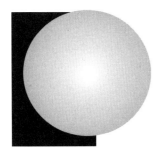

Introduction

Remember: Jung and Myers assumed that we use *all* of the mental functions at various times and for different reasons. So an interpretation that is appropriate to type looks at the type code as a reference to a *preferred* habit of mind rather than to the basic dimensions of the type as fixed traits. In other words, an individual might have a preference for Extraverted Thinking and also use Introverted Thinking, but these processes simply will not be used with the same level of awareness or pleasure. The logic in this illustration applies to all of the types.

How are type and leadership behaviors linked in these descriptions?

There is evidence to link each type to observed behaviors resulting in leader effectiveness and specific leader qualities. Rather than look just at individual type preferences such as extraversion or introversion, you will look at the *whole type dynamic* for each of the sixteen types. The research supporting this evidence is based on an extensive analysis of thousands of data points for the sixteen types. As you read about each of the types, keep in mind that links are being made with behaviors proven to be essential to leadership effectiveness and that these are based on hundreds of observations for each of the sixteen types.[5]

Observed Effectiveness

In general, effectiveness is defined as those qualities which others observe and *rate as effective*. While self-reported data are important and are provided in each type description, effectiveness and identified barriers to effectiveness of each type are based on extensive observational data.[6]

The focus of this guide is on the interpersonal qualities and skills which are central to getting the job done as a leader in an organization or of a team.[7] In addition to these qualities and as an indication of different kinds of business risks the types are generally willing to take, a brief discussion on Entrepreneurial Mindset for each type is presented.

Effectiveness Profiles

Each description includes:

- a review of the dynamics of that type
- typical expressions, general motivators
- insights people of the type have about their mental dynamics, but do not generally share
- blind spots that others see
- stress related behavior
- entrepreneurial mindset
- learning strategies, and
- an exemplary developmental quote from leaders of that type.

Introduction

The brief summary statements in each category provide a core description supported by research. Use these comments as guides for initiating exploration about the effects of your behavior, asking questions for clarification from others, and seeking additional feedback for leadership coaching purposes.

In research reporting on type and leadership *styles* (often labeled as delegating, coaching, or directing), the consistent finding is that there is no relationship between these styles and the sixteen types.[8] As the descriptions in this booklet reveal, each of the sixteen types has its own way to effectively delegate, direct, or encourage others.

A Learning Suggestion

The objective of this guide is to *acknowledge our gifts* and to *identify areas of growth*. If you slip into thinking "this is the way I am, I can't change," then this material has failed you. The useful perspective is "Here are my patterns of behavior, which I can sort into effective and ineffective. I need to acknowledge those things that are effective and find ways to continue using them. From those things that I do or do not do which diminish my effectiveness, I need to choose which ones I want to address and develop a plan for increasing my effectiveness."

Using this booklet as a teaching guide for self-development will aid you in enhancing your interpersonal endeavors. Your tasks as leader are:

- to learn to express qualities you have moderately developed, and

- to learn new capacities of expression which enhance your relationships.

Assuming you have made a decision to learn and grow, psychological type will provide you rich insights into your own leadership psychology and the needs of those who work with you as you serve in leadership roles.

MBTI Type

Dominant Function
with Auxiliary Function

On the following pages are descriptions of each type, presented using the categories outlined below:

Basic Habits of Mind

- Typical characteristics of the dominant and auxiliary mental functions (or processes).
- The combination of the natural extraverted and introverted cycle for each type is identified and its likely behavioral outcomes are presented.

Typical Communication Patterns

- When communicating, this type generally looks and sounds like the qualities listed here.
- Typical expressions are not the same as always behaving in a predicted way!

Motivated and Motivates Others By

- How this type directs and focuses energy toward getting things done.
- Special attention is paid to well-developed qualities of the type.

Observed Effective Behaviors

- Qualities identified as effective by direct reports, peers, and superiors.
- Behaviors related to teaming, self-management, and leader styles are listed.

Insights Rarely Shared

- Qualities that this type believes to be true but are rarely shared with others.
- Behaviors that this type believes to be true but that are not so clearly observed by others.

Blind Spots

- Qualities others often see that individuals of this type neither recognize nor acknowledge.
- Descriptors are based on differences among observers and individual self-ratings.

Potential Barriers to Effectiveness

- Qualities observers rate as problems for the type are listed.
- These are considered issues that could cause the type to stumble in organizations or be derailed from their career path.

MBTI Type

Dominant Function
with Auxiliary Function

Stress Related Behavior[9]

As a general introduction to this area, there is evidence that we rely on our most comfortable and easy to use skills, strategies, and processes in taking care of daily challenges. However, we initially exaggerate our dominant qualities when trying to respond to stressors in our life. With persistent stress, we will deplete our primary energies and leave room for the emergence of the least consciously used function of our type. The least used function is often called the "Inferior Function," but it is only inferior in our awareness of it. *It is not inferior in strength or potential.*

- The initial stress response—doing more of what we already do.
- The response with persistent, unrelenting stress.
- The demonstrated type behaviors when stress becomes distress.

Entrepreneurial Mindset

- Descriptors of the activities and attitudes of this type in the entrepreneurial setting are listed here.
- The primary areas of interest for starting a "new business" are listed. *These may be encouraged inside, as well as external to, an organization.*

General Learning Strategy

- How the individuals of this type go about learning and adjusting to new behaviors.
- Brief descriptors of learning strategies employed.
- Suggestions on how to enhance learning for the given type.

Exemplary Development Comment by Leaders of Each Type

- Executives and managers were asked about their key insights into their effectiveness, given their type.
- These are exact quotes from leaders after being introduced to type.
- Special comments are summarized concerning what might need to be done or might be overdone in their leadership roles.

Sixteen
MBTI
Profiles

Introverted Sensing

    With Extraverted Thinking   ISTJ

    With Extraverted Feeling   ISFJ

Introverted Intuition

    With Extraverted Thinking   INTJ

    With Extraverted Feeling   INFJ

Introverted Thinking

    With Extraverted Sensing   ISTP

    With Extraverted Intuition   INTP

Introverted Feeling

    With Extraverted Sensing   ISFP

    With Extraverted Intuition   INFP

Extraverted Sensing

    With Introverted Thinking   ESTP

    With Introverted Feeling   ESFP

Extraverted Intuition

    With Introverted Thinking   ENTP

    With Introverted Feeling   ENFP

Extraverted Thinking

    With Introverted Sensing   ESTJ

    With Introverted Intuition   ENTJ

Extraverted Feeling

    With Introverted Sensing   ESFJ

    With Introverted Intuition   ENFJ

Introverted
Sensing

with Extraverted Thinking

Basic Habits of Mind

ISTJ leaders seek precision and clarity in spoken or written information. These two qualities promote a thorough and practical concentration on the task at hand. With Introverted Sensing as the lead mental process, ISTJs have an immediate, concrete focus on the here and now. With an Extraverted Thinking auxiliary, they are likely to appear as focused, orderly, critical, and decisive people who trust facts and structure.

Typical Communication Patterns

- Careful in spoken communication to share tested and verifiable data.
- Calm and unassuming, they seem decisive, predictable, and realistic in their expression of information.
- Expect a logical, matter-of-fact conversation from ISTJs because of the role of extraverted thinking.

Motivated and Motivates By

- Attempt to motivate others with precise, accurate, and timely information.
- Description of situations followed by a concise, analytical observation is made with an assumption that logical order will engage others.

Observed Effective Behaviors

- Straightforward communication and the capacity to confront difficult people who behave in inappropriate ways.
- Being fair-minded, organized, and decisive are seen as typical qualities.

Insights Rarely Shared

- They see themselves as less expressive than other types. They believe this quality makes them least likely to become over-dependent on others and have difficulty with management direction for the organization.
- Often feel they carry an unusual load of responsibility within a group.

Blind Spots

- Others may consider the deliberate analytical behavior of ISTJs as manipulating, demanding, and impatient.
- They are often seen as pressuring and blunt.
- ISTJs might be surprised to learn that their commitment to careful precision is interpreted by some as guarded dogmatism.
- Their decisiveness can come across as blunt, opinionated views.

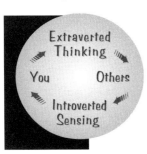

Introverted Sensing

with Extraverted Thinking

Potential Barriers to Effectiveness

- ISTJs need to learn to create a more developmental climate and demonstrate more compassion for those who work with them.
- Having a low tolerance for ambiguity, they sometimes find it difficult to advance in organizations where a teamwork orientation is essential.

Stress Related Behavior

- Often attempt to manage stress through methodological strategies and getting things done; this becomes exaggerated to look like a person insisting on control and conformance to expectations.
- Under enough stress, their natural attention to precision becomes excessive. Energy is spent on anticipating the failure and the incompetence of people and processes around them.

Entrepreneurial Mindset

- Having a high need to achieve within the structure of organizations, they are often the "worker bees" of industry.
- When they open a business, it is an extension of their already heavily used talents in the workplace. For example, if an ISTJ is an accountant for the EXK Corporation, he or she might open a small tax service in the evenings or on weekends. If starting a business, ISTJs are drawn to practical activities like retail or electrical industries.

General Learning Strategy

- Learn best with clearly stated objectives and procedures, prefer to analyze, examine, and think-it-through before telling others.
- Learning strategies employed: analyzing, identifying factual accuracy first, labeling and categorizing information.
- Learning enhanced by clear directions, pre-work with "doing" activities such as answering questions, engaging in some competitive challenge.

Exemplary Development Comment

- "The results that are gained from my work tend to reinforce what I consider effective, but I tend to bruise people. I have rarely considered other approaches which I need to do."
- "I need to learn that 'fairness' is different for everyone and not treat everyone the same. I tend to delegate well but need to become more effective at encouraging and coaching others."

Introverted Sensing

with Extraverted Feeling

Basic Habits of Mind

As leaders, ISFJs tend to be realistic, calm, consistent, and careful with facts. Loyal and reliable, they trust their experience and the consistency of information. With Introverted Sensing as their lead function, ISFJs have a storehouse of memories and facts. Their auxiliary Extraverted Feeling leads to cooperative, sympathetic, and affiliative behaviors. Experienced as warm and thoughtful, they express interest in people rather than things.

Typical Communication Patterns

- Often do what they believe will be helpful to others without asserting their own needs.
- Due to their precise and focused attention to the world around them, they may give relatively unhurried interest and concern to others.
- They are careful to achieve balance in their work and personal life and assume others do so as well, being careful to get the job done before the deadline so as to prevent stressful, last-minute effort.

Motivated and Motivates Others By

- Enthusiastic about organized and concise information.
- Check out the facts before taking action, especially as related to helping others.
- They often feel that if you show and tell, then you will get people to understand the job that needs to be done.

Observed Effective Behaviors

- Being sensitive and compassionate to others are expressed behaviors of ISFJs.
- ISFJs have a strong cooperative orientation. They are seen as dependable and expressive of appreciation.
- Relationship building and sensitivity to others are seen as positive and effective expressions common to ISFJs.

Insights Rarely Shared

- See themselves as straightforward, flexible, easy-to-get-along-with kind of people.
- Do what is necessary and sufficient to get the job done without seeking the limelight and want to lead by example.

Blind Spots

- Seen as pragmatically resourceful, this type sometimes appears to be unaware they are so conventional as to be self-centered, abrupt, and uncompromising.

Introverted Sensing

with Extraverted Feeling

- They would be surprised to learn that their behaviors could be seen as stingy, overly conventional, and rigid.

Potential Barriers to Effectiveness

- Becoming over-dependent on structures and standard operating procedures, being over-controlled, and having difficulty with staff relationships.
- Their lack of interest in the limelight means that they often do not get their views aired and if they are not careful, they may behave in ways that diminish the social presence needed to influence others.

Stress Related Behavior

- Become exceptionally conventional and reserved and may appear unemotional, stingy with time and resources, and demanding.
- When the stress is great enough, they see evidence in the smallest events that the future is dark and is unlikely to be enjoyable.
- Under extreme stress, they may actually seem impulsive and unrealistic in their expectations.

Entrepreneurial Mindset

- Less likely to leave the structure and conformity of organizational life; small business activity is related to hands-on, practical services for others.
- May have a weekend business and take early retirement to foster a small service-related business such as in-home practical care for injured or elderly, part time investigative or safety services, or small booking-for-hire service.

General Learning Strategy

- Visual learners, prefer "show and tell," seeing a video, reading cases that are illustrative of the points being made.
- Learning strategies employed: observing, graphing, organizing, applying.
- Learning enhanced by small group, cooperative learning discussions that focus on personal experiences.

Exemplary Development Comment by Leader

- "The fact that I am reserved and casual leads me to be less forceful than I may need to be in certain situations. The higher I go in the organization, the more forceful, assertive, and initiating I need to become."
- "I tend to rely too much on skills I use easily and well. I do not socialize enough with diverse personalities and I do not give people enough information about the task I am working on...I assume it is obvious."

Introverted
Intuition

Basic Habits of Mind

INTJs as leaders are analytical and innovative. The lead function for INTJs is Introverted Intuition which immediately recognizes the complexity of ideas and possibilities. Often seeing relationships among apparently unrelated events or facts, introverted intuition provides for an uncanny awareness of situations. Supporting this awareness is the auxiliary Extraverted Thinking process that navigates the environment with analytical and critical precision.

Typical Communication Patterns

- Because extraverted thinking is used as a primary mode of engaging people, INTJs often seem questioning and skeptical.
- A collector of theories and ideas, INTJs find a model to make sense of most any situation.
- Expressively logical, orderly, and systematic evaluations are typical of INTJs.
- Intensity is apparent during interactions. This is the result of the difficulty in appropriately and efficiently expressing all of the complexity which introverted intuition has perceived.

Motivated and Motivates By

- Appreciate and are responsive to mental versatility, systematic analysis, and high aspirations.
- Explaining overall framework for action, by connecting actions, motives, and outcomes, and by providing a "formula" about their experiences.

Observed Effective Behaviors

- Observers feel INTJs are a quick study, are independent-minded, and are interested in power and influence.
- Being deliberate, forceful, and demanding are also effective qualities of INTJs.

Insights Rarely Shared

- INTJs feel flexible, self-aware, tolerant, and decisive.
- INTJs often feel that others see them as absorbed in a task and intentionally excluding others, though that is not their intent.

Blind Spots

- Often unaware that their decisive, analytical style appears dogmatic, impatient, and manipulating, INTJs could learn from continuous feedback about the effects of their interpersonal style.
- Their independence and critical-mindedness are often interpreted as having difficulty with upper management decisions or strategic directions.

INTJ

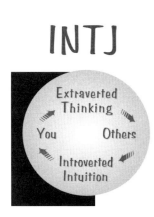

Introverted
Intuition

with Extraverted Thinking

Potential Barriers to Effectiveness

- They need to strengthen relationships, to demonstrate more compassion and sensitivity, and to be careful about disagreements with management decisions.
- For INTJs, what feels like open, direct communication which is honest and sensitive, and clear, critical questions about decisions being made, is experienced by others as being opinionated, detached, and manipulative.

Stress Related Behavior

- Increasing skepticism and broader questioning is reflective of increasing levels of stress for INTJs. They may appear to be very hard-headed and condescending.
- When the pressure is great enough, they may become obsessed with a fact that is then distorted beyond all reasonable recognition.
- More likely, however, is that they become obsessed with hair-splitting precision that no one can match.

Entrepreneurial Mindset

- They envision themselves as entrepreneurs because of their drive for independence and control.
- Significant independent achievers, when they are on their own, they often provide consulting services.
- They feel they see the "big picture" and can provide comprehensive business services such as HR planning and legal services, computer innovations, and international business strategies.

General Learning Strategy

- Prefer to learn about global issues first, to envision possibilities, to speculate, and to actively make connections between ideas.
- Learning strategies employed: independent analysis, debating, researching a problem, connecting experience to abstraction or model.
- Learning enhanced by pursuing open-ended questions, providing time for analysis before discussing, allowing freedom to brainstorm and design.

Exemplary Development Comment

- "I overdo concepts and do not pay enough attention to data, leading to judgments that are too quick. I need to be more inclusive of others and show appreciation. I need to analyze less, gather data more."

Introverted Intuition

with Extraverted Feeling

Basic Habits of Mind

INFJ leaders perceive the complexity of interpersonal relationships and circumstances of situations with clarity. The lead mental function of Introverted Intuition links inspiration, ideals, and imagination. The auxiliary Extraverted Feeling function drives the type to engage with other people and to evaluate the events around them with an awareness of the consequences on people and treasured ideals.

Typical Communication Patterns

- Appreciative of others' efforts. Attentive and sensitive to the emergence of various qualities and dynamics during interactions with others.
- They put special emphasis on personal frameworks for decisions.
- Often warm, cooperative, and sympathetic.
- Expressive of their inner vision and engage others so they can connect with this vision.

Motivated and Motivates By

- INFJs motivate others using cooperation and by acting on values which promote human well-being.
- Inclusive of others, put energy into tasks and activities which reflect on their values for establishing enduring relationships.

Observed Effective Behaviors

- Demonstrated behaviors which build a developmental climate, put others at ease, show independence of thought are seen as effective in organizations.
- The casual, easy-going interpersonal style of this type is seen as an effective way to be demanding, straightforward, and deliberate.

Insights Rarely Shared

- They think of themselves as very compassionate, sensitive, and empathetic with others.
- They see themselves as decisive and responsible in their behaviors toward others.

INFJ

Blind Spots

- While generally seen as resourceful, INFJs are surprised to learn that others see overdependence in relationships, undeveloped criteria for hiring staff, and not enough social presence to have the influence needed to change situations in organizations.
- They are often surprised to learn that others see their style as being unsupportive of management initiatives.

Introverted
Intuition

with Extraverted Feeling

Potential Barriers to Effectiveness

- Interpersonal style may be seen as guarded and pressuring.
- These qualities undermine trust and a feeling of fair play when dealing with the boss.
- INFJs need to be careful that their empathy and demonstrated interest in fostering relationships are not translated as permissive.

Stress Related Behavior

- Increasing cautious and "reserved" behaviors may be signs of stress.
- They may appear to be dreamy and retiring, and express unrealistic expectations as stress increases.
- If the stresses are persistent, INFJs might exhibit a relentless concern about details of the day as more meaningful than they really are. This obsession with current events and how these are related to the "sorry condition of the world" indicate the stressors need to be reduced.

Entrepreneurial Mindset

- When they set up companies or organizations, they generally plan a small organization with specific service related work.
- They enjoy independence and seek opportunities that allow freedom to blossom.
- As new business operators they often articulate the vision well, especially as related to educational consulting, running an art gallery, or becoming a media specialist.

General Learning Strategy

- INFJs think about things in unique ways before acting on ideas, seek to clarify with open-ended questions.
- Learning strategies employed: writing about it before talking about it, illustrating ideas, using cooperative learning simulations.
- Learning enhanced by small group discussions, creating supportive climate, opportunities to elaborate and change point of view.

Exemplary Development Comment

- "I enjoy ideas and possibilities so much that I often overlook the details of what needs to be practically done to make an idea real. While I am good with people, I often do not demonstrate enough analytical ability for others to take me seriously."
- "While I am excellent with people situations, I am not so accomplished with conflictual discussions. I need to see conflict as a source of ideas."

Introverted Thinking

with Extraverted Sensing

Basic Habits of Mind

ISTPs lead by being analytical. This produces a decisive and incisive perspective concerned with precision and exactness. Introverted Thinking pulls this type to be reflective, skeptical, and critical. Aided by Extraverted Sensing which provides an acute awareness of the present situation, Introverted Thinking is adaptable as long as logical order can be made out of the situation.

Typical Communication Patterns

- General initial reaction to ISTPs is that they are reflective, but when engaged they are quick on their feet, quite ingenious, and realistic in their remarks.
- Seen as good-natured, when they are talking they know the who, what, where, and when of situations.

Motivated and Motivates By

- Motivated by dealing with practical concerns.
- They want to get things done that are consonant with their experience and framework for a situation.
- They enjoy analyzing their world and are motivated to engage in critical discussion as long as the outcome has specific results.
- Tangible goals get the "juices moving."

Observed Effective Behaviors

- Straightforward, resourceful, fair, and consenting are among the highest rated qualities.
- Being able to accurately identify the individual strengths and capabilities of those who work with them.

Insights Rarely Shared

- ISTPs feel decisive about *and* flexible to new ideas.
- They believe they are able to confront others effectively and quickly.
- ISTPs believe their attention to the details of the moment contributes to a developmental climate for others.

Blind Spots

- ISTPs are sometimes seen as blunt, detached, guarded, impersonal and low on demonstrated empathy.
- While they think of themselves as able to competently maneuver social settings, their social behavior often fails to make the impression they imagined was true.

ISTP

Introverted Thinking

with Extraverted Sensing

Potential Barriers to Effectiveness

- Making strategic transitions during organizational change.
- In environments where change is frequent, they may discover their logical, critical comments are perceived as disagreeing with upper management.

Stress Related Behavior

- As stress increases, ISTPs often seem more restless and non-conforming.
- The critical, analytical, logical expressions become increasingly intense due to the prolonged self-imposed silence they show during stress.
- When the stressors last long enough and with enough intensity, ISTPs become unusually sensitive to people's verbal and nonverbal behavior, seeing rejection and disregard in the simplest of events.

Entrepreneurial Mindset

- They enjoy small businesses that provide a specific, practical, hands-on type of service.
- They may hire several others but do not plan to grow beyond a medium sized company in technical areas such as electrical, mechanical, safety, and security.
- Many start a specialized carpentry shop or technically related organization.
- Once they develop their expertise, they are more likely to lease their operations to others of the same interests rather than develop a large organization.

General Learning Strategy

- Learn while actively "doing," actively experimenting with ideas.
- Learning strategies employed: demonstrations of ideas, analyses in the moment, creating structure and order, adapting to "current best model."
- Learning enhanced by structure and variety, clearly stated competency goals.

Exemplary Development Comment

- "I prefer to take action. This orientation along with my determination gets misread as not being a team player. I need to gain a greater depth of understanding about situations. I superficially listen to things I deem irrelevant when in fact they may become very important later on."
- "As I overdo acting and thinking, I don't spend enough time on feelings and including others. My effectiveness will be greatly hampered until I focus on these human interaction factors."

Introverted Thinking

with Extraverted Intuition

Basic Habits of Mind

INTPs lead by seeking answers to questions in terms of the causes, outcomes, and variable relationships of people, places, and things. Analytical and logical, INTPs have Introverted Thinking as a primary function, which is aided in its analysis with the patterns perceived by Extraverted Intuition. The auxiliary Extraverted Intuition is in tune with the complexity in the environment. An awareness of the fluidity of situations is often a hallmark of this function.

Typical Communication Patterns

- INTPs enjoy presenting the most recent theory or model of interest to explain their experiences.
- They see paradox and irony in almost everything they do, which leads to unconventional and imaginative remarks.
- They are autonomous problem solvers and are willing to validate their analysis of events through conversation when invited to do so.

Motivated and Motivates By

- INTPs are motivated by intellectual and complex challenges.
- The tougher the problem, the greater their interest.
- They gain a great deal of energy from talking about theoretical models and find debate invigorating.

Observed Effective Behaviors

- Seen as decisive and as a quick study given most situations, they are also seen as casual, independent-minded, and initiating.
- Aware that when they delegate they are effective, they often seek ways to communicate both understanding and urgency when dealing with others.

Insights Rarely Shared

- INTPs think that being mindful of concepts and theories gives them flexibility and an understanding of interpersonal interdependence.
- As leaders their careful, moderate approach to others leads to a belief that they are good at building interpersonal relations.

Blind Spots

- INTPs would be surprised to learn that they do not put people at ease as quickly as they imagine.
- They may appear pressuring, blunt, impatient, and as having difficulty with follow-through.
- As a result of these occasional qualities, INTPs have more staff relationship issues than they initially think.

Introverted Thinking

with Extraverted Intuition

Potential Barriers to Effectiveness

- Learning to build and mend peer and direct report relationships is critical to the future success of INTPs.
- If they do not learn the lessons of encouraging others and interpersonal warmth, then others will see them as having poor work team commitment and a poor confrontation record.

Stress Related Behavior

- As stress increases, INTPs become more restless and defensive.
- They critically analyze the big picture which feeds the urgency to solve the problem. This leads to a forceful and sometimes rebellious action because "no one else can grasp the scope of the problem."
- With sufficient stress, this type becomes hypersensitive and expressive of disappointment in the lack of care others show for his or her cause.

Entrepreneurial Mindset

- Their ideal might be a one-person show involved with a technical proficiency.
- An example of the kind of new business activity INTPs might develop is starting up an editing company (of one or two employees) to help company newsletters improve the quality of research writing and editing for scientific communities.

General Learning Strategy

- Prefer lots of freedom to explore, insist on variety of tasks and creative opportunities for learning and testing theories.
- Learning strategies employed: analyzing "it" first before actually testing it, comparing and contrasting with other experiences, critiquing.
- Learning enhanced by providing intellectual challenges, opportunities to write or illustrate abstractions, clarify through elaborate analysis.

Exemplary Development Comment

- "I am too methodical and too unwilling to open up to suggestions and thoughts of others. People have a hard time figuring me out. I need to strengthen my listening skills."
- "I sometimes react in a manner that can easily swing my analytical strengths into weaknesses when dealing with others. As a leader in the organization, it is clear that I need to strengthen my interaction skills to be more effective."

Introverted Feeling

with Extraverted Sensing

Basic Habits of Mind

ISFPs are gentle leaders who make decisions based on their ideals and web of relationships as well as a desire to take practical action. Introverted Feeling leads ISFPs to find supportive environments and to develop strong though few interpersonal relationships. Aided by Extraverted Sensing as the auxiliary, this type is aware of the immediate, present situation in which they find themselves. The auxiliary leads to a reliable awareness of the practical considerations of any decisions that are being made.

Typical Communication Patterns

- Because of the reflective, deferent nature of ISFPs, their typical expressions are factually brief, good-natured, and concise.
- They show their intentions and real commitments more by actions than by words.
- In their conversation, they know the who, what, where, and when of people and situations, which they believe is evidence of truly caring about others and situations.

Motivated and Motivates By

- ISFPs get excited by taking practical action to help people.
- They gently encourage others to act and they quietly act to address an issue or situation.
- Personal, matter-of-fact, hands-on assistance enthuses them.

Observed Effective Behaviors

- ISFPs are seen as resourceful, flexible, and teamwork-oriented.
- These are qualities which contribute to the perception that they are good at building relationships and promoting a developmental climate.
- Others observe that when they are blunt, methodical, and pressuring, they are often effective at leading others.

Insights Rarely Shared

- Most people would be surprised to learn that ISFPs have a strong belief that they do what must be done to get the job done, and that they are direct and straightforward in their communications.
- They often feel they are a quick study, though others may not immediately see this quality.

Blind Spots

- Others perceive that this type is overdependent on a select few, and not concerned enough with making a good impression as being socially involved.
- Relative to others, ISFPs are unaware of how their deferent behavior may be seen as merely "going along."

Introverted Feeling

with Extraverted Sensing

Potential Barriers to Effectiveness

- Seen as guarded and impatient at times.
- Observers would like to see a demonstration of more strategic-mindedness.
- While often good with their direct reports and bosses, ISFPs have unusual difficulty in getting their peers to appreciate the gifts brought to the table.

Stress Related Behavior

- When stressed, ISFPs become undependable in follow-through and suspicious of others' intentions.
- Under enough prolonged stress, ISFPs become hypercritical of others and find an endless list of reasons for the unacceptability of some action or fact.
- A skeptical, touchy interpersonal style will emerge during stressful times.

Entrepreneurial Mindset

- If they start up an operation, it is likely to be a service that meets personal needs, such as a counseling, nutritional center, or custom carpentry.
- Usually, their start-up operations move slowly and only take on a few people. If it grows too fast or too large, they are eager to sell out.

General Learning Strategy

- Prefer opportunities to work cooperatively with a small group, will concretely test ideas, and prefer to do things that have personal meaning.
- Learning strategies employed: taking time to find personal connections in experiences, relating to personal values, and producing concrete results.
- Learning enhanced by tasks that have personal connection, opportunities to identify rather than create models or categories of information.

Exemplary Development Comment

- "I grasp facts quickly and given time can bring in the big picture. While I often involve others in a process, they may not perceive me as knowing what I'm looking for."
- "I am easygoing and patient because I do not like being distracted with emotions. I like to operate in crisis situations because my calm and easygoing demeanor is a strength."

Introverted Feeling

with Extraverted Intuition

Basic Habits of Mind

INFPs as leaders seek congruence between their ideals and the current situation. With a dominant Introverted Feeling function, INFPs make decisions by looking at the consequences on people and how outcomes will fit into their values and ideals. Aided by Extraverted Intuition which seeks out possibilities and patterns, this type makes connections among people, ideas, and events and then evaluates their acceptability.

Typical Communication Patterns

- INFPs discuss possible future actions and ask open questions to "get along".
- The interconnections they see often lead to some unconventional speculation about situations.
- They often give carefully worded summaries of their thoughts and ideas.

Motivated and Motivates By

- Motivated by autonomy and complexity in situations.
- Introspective and gentle, they are often eager to be adaptable and encourage others to do likewise to enhance motivation.
- Creatively finding room to generate alternate solutions to problems.
- Will put a great deal of energy into actualizing personal values.

Observed Effective Behaviors

- Seen as effective when they are expressing compassion, building relationships, demonstrating changeability, and encouraging others.
- Observers indicate that INFPs are very good at creating a developmental work climate.

Insights Rarely Shared

- INFPs perceive themselves as very able team members and very competent at selecting talented people with whom to work.
- They often feel that they cannot completely share their insights due to the complexity of interrelationships they see.

Blind Spots

- INFPs are unlikely to recognize that they appear to be overdependent on a select group, unconcerned with making a good impression, and too reserved to be effective.
- Not following through in a timely manner is sometimes an issue.

Potential Barriers to Effectiveness

- Sometimes seen as guarded, detached, impatient, dogmatic,

Introverted Feeling

with Extraverted Intuition

and opinionated.

- Their reserved nature leads to a lack of sociability that gives people discomfort.

Stress Related Behavior

- INFPs get surprised with how touchy and unrealistic they become when they are under stress.
- They become noticeably distracted and impulsive as the stress increases.
- With continued stress, they will become very critical and petty, seeming harsh and very negative toward others and themselves.

Entrepreneurial Mindset

- When they start up an operation, it is usually directed to social or environmental causes. They often are in art, writing, and counseling-related endeavors.
- INFPs would be interested in starting up a stock brokerage that handles environmentally sensitive companies or training firms focused on helping people manage diversity.

General Learning Strategy

- Prefer to engage in holistic models and frameworks when learning, need to see how the learning will be valuable to life mission and goals.
- Learning strategies employed: journal writing, attending seminars, and opportunities for creative expression.
- Learning enhanced by providing minimal structure with a few open-ended questions, role plays or other simulations, non-competitive situations.

Exemplary Development Comment

- "I am so determined to get my unit to work toward my ideal that I am sometimes too demanding and have expectations that are too high. I don't always share clearly enough what I am expecting from others which leads to frustrations for them and for me. I tend to overcompensate for my preference toward collaboration and inward focus by being overly directive, blunt, and demanding."
- "I sometimes let my concerns for people influence my decision-making, which is not necessarily a bad thing; I just need to demonstrate more analytical skills, and to show others that I am concerned about basic business issues. I just don't try to influence people enough and persuade them to a new point of view. I need to solicit more feedback and network with others more."

Extraverted Sensing

with Introverted Thinking

Basic Habits of Mind

ESTPs as leaders are so acutely aware of the environment and people that they respond quickly and adaptively. In tune with the immediate situation, their lead function of Extraverted Sensing is focused on concrete, exact facts which promote expedient action. With Introverted Thinking as the auxiliary, ESTPs are busy fitting information into logical frameworks in order to made sense of experience. Due to the dominant process, the Introverted Thinking aspects of ESTPs lead to quick analysis and action.

Typical Communication Patterns

- Energetic, fast paced communicators who enjoy whatever is useful to do at the moment.
- Good-natured and realistic in their interactions.
- Often good at easing tensions due to their sense of humor, they are also very critical and analytical when exploring situations.
- Actively seek facts which then lead to concise questions of others.
- Sometimes their inaction is in fact their analytical reflection looking for the quickest, shortest route between two points.

Motivated and Motivates By

- Being on the move, focusing on the present, and quickly acting to efficiently solve problems motivate ESTPs.
- Being on the "emergency team" or the "disaster recovery team."

Observed Effective Behaviors

- Confronting difficult employees effectively, asserting points of view.
- Being decisive and deliberate.
- Having considerable social presence that is persuasive.

Insights Rarely Shared

- ESTPs often believe they have compassion for others, are being strategic-minded, and work well on teams.
- They spend more time keeping balance in their life than others recognize.

Blind Spots

- ESTPs believe themselves to be more resourceful and interpersonally responsible than others see.
- They are sometimes seen as noncommittal, detached, and abrasive.

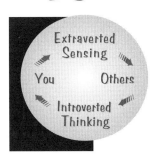

Extraverted
Sensing

with Introverted Thinking

Potential Barriers to Effectiveness

- Failure to actively demonstrate a commitment to a developmental climate in the workplace by being as empathetic as they are critical.
- Failure to take the time to show their interest in the long-range strategic future of the organization.

Stress Related Behavior

- When in a pinch, ESTPs appear opportunistic, restless, and unkind.
- They will become more aggressive in seeking information and forceful in expecting people to conform.
- Under enough persistent stress, they may seem inwardly obsessed with what they believe are probable and dire possibilities.
- They convince themselves that they know just how terrible a situation is before checking it out with someone.

Entrepreneurial Mindset

- High-energy individuals who like to start companies that provide a necessary, hands-on product or service.
- They enjoy the challenge of making the sale. ESTPs will start up operations when they have a team of people who will take care of all the details and procedures. Their businesses are often marketing related or in a specialized consulting area such as detective work, law enforcement, or trade marketing.

General Learning Strategy

- Prefer quick paced, analytical, and challenging opportunities to learn.
- Learning strategies employed: active testing of ideas, constructing answers in-the-moment rather than analyzing reflectively.
- Like being physically active.
- Learning enhanced by competitive opportunities, clear instructions, socializing.

Exemplary Development Comment

- "I am competitive to a fault. I need to show more appreciation. I am often impatient when people are telling me things I already know and then proceed to 'write them off' and exclude them. In fact, those people are crucial to my later success."
- "Ability to think and analyze so quickly leads to me not doing my homework and being somewhat incomplete in my review of a situation. My preset analysis leads to putting more weight on some information and less on others when it should be the other way around. I am fast moving but I'm learning that not everyone else is fast in the same way."

Extraverted Sensing

with Introverted Feeling

Basic Habits of Mind

ESFPs as leaders are friendly, practical, and responsive. Their dominant Extraverted Sensing leads to easy connections with people and people-related things in their environment. They have a quick awareness of the human dynamics of a situation. Eager to enjoy the moment, ESFPs seek out novel experiences. Aided by Introverted Feeling, ESFPs use this judgment process for deciding the acceptability of circumstances and the way to approach people. These qualities make it easy for them to move among many different types of people and situations.

Typical Communication Patterns

- They naturally express concern for and enjoyment of others.
- Their comments are generally focused on the here and now.
- They enjoy conversation and are easily engaged on most any topic of current interest.
- They are actively involved in interactions, putting a great deal of energy into being inclusive and being included by others.

Motivated and Motivates By

- Physical activity and by focusing on problems of a practical nature.
- Working in teams and find immediate action more satisfying than long-term goal setting, though they see the need for it.
- Engaging with others at a personal level that gets them involved in the situation in front of them.

Observed Effective Behaviors

- Compassionate nature, sensitivity, and social flexibility.
- Easygoing manner enables them to be demanding and pressuring in effective ways.
- Putting people at ease and putting forth ideas and persuading others to listen.

Insights Rarely Shared

- ESFPs often think they are very straightforward and effective at leading others.
- They see themselves as resourceful and decisive.

Blind Spots

- Many ESFPs would be surprised to learn that others see them as overdependent on a select group and slightly less self-controlled than other people.
- They would be surprised to learn that their quick responsiveness and easygoing manner is interpreted by some as noncommittal (having simply "reacted"), impatient, and pressuring.

Extraverted Sensing

with Introverted Feeling

Potential Barriers to Effectiveness

- When they appear impatient, noncommittal, and blunt, ESFPs are viewed as ineffective.
- They need to show that they will do what is needed to get the job done and that they can be a quick study.

Stress Related Behavior

- They seem to be undependable, touchy, and rigid when under stress.
- They may appear opportunistic and abrupt as stress increases.
- With too much stress, they will become reserved and guarded, and they find themselves imagining the worst possible outcomes of the situation they are in.

Entrepreneurial Mindset

- Their natural thrill of getting things done in the moment leads ESFPs to start up retail operations where they work with the public and see their business grow with each sale.
- While they like working on practical matters, they greatly enjoy the front line customer—business activity needed for the product to move. Some of their businesses include childcare, transportation, designer, and consumer-goods-related industries.

General Learning Strategy

- Prefer to learn by using concrete activities or objects to illustrate ideas, like to be involved with cooperative learning opportunities.
- Learning strategies employed: creating groups to explore information, may "act it out" to see others' reactions, sharing personal meaning of experience.
- Learning enhanced by telling stories, visual aids, and concrete information.

Exemplary Development Comment

- "I tend to overdo the acting and underdo the thinking. As a result, I am impulsive and impatient. I want to complete the task NOW!"
- "I need to reflect on situations, then construct an organized plan of action. I need to actively listen, show more patience, and recognize that the process may be as valuable as the task in order to lead others for the future."

Extraverted Intuition

with Introverted Thinking

Basic Habits of Mind

ENTPs as leaders focus on future possibilities that are related to present circumstances. The dominant process for ENTPs, Extraverted Intuition, seeks out patterns and interrelationships among ideas and frameworks. Introverted Thinking serves as an auxiliary process to make decisions about information and situations. Questioning and skeptical, ENTPs' decisions are continuously flowing from introverted thinking as they seek to make sense of their experiences.

Typical Communication Patterns

- Why, when, and "why not" are typical questions of ENTPs.
- They enjoy pushing ideas and getting reactions, to "stir the pot."
- Verbally fluent and fast paced in their communications, ENTPs are action oriented.
- Relatively uninhibited, they are eager to ask almost any question to "follow their nose."

Motivated and Motivates By

- Situations which encourage their independent mindedness and challenge their problem-solving skills. They want to be fully competent and cutting edge.
- They are inclined to become somewhat detached and try to see the "whole" as a way to increase their energy when dealing with a situation.

Observed Effective Behaviors

- Seen as effective at being a quick study, being assertive, putting their ideas out to persuade others, and doing what it takes to reach the goal.
- While they are socially able to work with most any group, their social effectiveness increases with their casual, interpersonal style.

Insights Rarely Shared

- They see themselves as resourceful, self-aware, flexible, and very able at creating developmental climates in the workplace.
- Their perception of their abilities to achieve these qualities is related to their adaptability to experience.

Blind Spots

- They would be surprised to learn that their questioning seems impulsive, pressuring, critical, and opinionated at times.
- Observers note concern about their limited degree of expressed compassion for others, ability to build relationships on teams, and ability to constructively confront others.

ENTP

Extraverted Intuition

with Introverted Thinking

- Others observe that ENTP flexibility interferes with the implementation of plans and actions.

Potential Barriers to Effectiveness

- Some see their analytical questioning as a noncommittal and overly critical behavior.
- Seen as impatient with those who do not think as quickly, and appear unconcerned about their work/personal life balance.

Stress Related Behavior

- Stressful events can lead them to become more questioning and forceful in getting answers.
- They can become impulsive, unrealistic, hasty, and noisy as their stress increases.
- After prolonged stressful events or situations, they become very quiet and reserved as they focus on some fact or incident. This focus becomes an obsessive concern about a fact and its meaning, usually resulting in a negative self-interpretation.

Entrepreneurial Mindset

- They generally feel they are good company starters in marketing, photography, systems (computer), and consulting.
- They enjoy the challenge of making a business work from day to day as long as they do not have to attend to the details of the business.
- While they love to make sure the balance sheets are accurate and timely, their primary satisfaction is in making ideas real.

General Learning Strategy

- Prefer lots of variety in learning tasks, like to debate, link ideas quickly.
- Learning strategies employed: questioning, evaluating, synthesizing.
- Learning enhanced by providing a global picture of what is to be learned and by allowing active critical analysis of learning objectives and tasks.

Exemplary Development Comment

- "Perfectionism has become an obsession with me. I may not have risked failure, shutting out some possibilities merely because I can't do them perfectly. I am also critical and demanding of others, often leading me to reject solutions just because I don't think they are correct. I not only need to listen, but to understand."
- "I think through a problem well and jump to solve the problem a little too quickly. This doesn't allow others to give their input. I need to be more patient, less questioning, and more appreciative in leading others."

Extraverted Intuition

with Introverted Feeling

Basic Habits of Mind

Driven to new ideas and possibilities, ENFPs as leaders like "going with the flow." Their dominant process, Extraverted Intuition, seeks to connect current experience to future possible outcomes. Their active imagination is triggered by external events. This is aided by Introverted Feeling which provides a decisive judgment about the acceptability of problems in a situation. Drawn toward people and people related concerns, Introverted Feeling works toward understanding relationships in context.

Typical Communication Patterns

- ENFPs express enthusiasm about ideas and about being with people.
- They openly reveal their observations and reactions to situations.
- Eager to discuss the big picture, their language is expansive and filled with remarks about future possibilities.
- Warmth and concern for others often come through their activities as they enjoy engaging others in almost any task.

Motivated and Motivates By

- They are motivated by opportunities to share ideas, brainstorm, and engage with others to solve personal problems.
- Flexible environments which encourage innovation and looking for new connections among experiences and ideas are great motivators for this type.

Observed Effective Behaviors

- Rated among the highest in creating developmental climates, building and mending relationships, expressing compassion and empathy, this type is seen as effective in leading groups in problem solving and conflict resolution.
- They are usually effective at being adaptable, energetic, and appreciative.

Insights Rarely Shared

- They think of themselves as unusually resourceful and quick minded.
- They feel they are flexible and are effective work team members.

Blind Spots

- They would be surprised to learn that observers see them as somewhat overdependent on a small group of insiders, somewhat low in self-control, needing to be more straightforward and to follow through more completely.

ENFP

Extraverted Intuition

with Introverted Feeling

Potential Barriers to Effectiveness

- They need to learn more constructive confrontation, to be more demonstrative of support for upper management strategy, and more deliberate in their management of tasks.
- When their values are pinched, they seem guarded, dogmatic, and hypersensitive, which interferes with their effectiveness.

Stress Related Behavior

- Stressors often result in this type increasing tempo, becoming more active in reacting to situations, and very talkative.
- They become more impulsive, hasty, noisy, and distracted as stress increases.
- With enough persistent stress, they may become very quiet while they focus on a fact or two and obsess about its meaning (usually in very negative ways).

Entrepreneurial Mindset

- In businesses where teamwork is required to get it off the ground, ENFPs are a natural.
- More often than not, they are willing to let others handle specific business issues (like accounting and contracts) while they rally the troops to expand the company.
- They are drawn to service related industries such as artistic services, training, executive coaching, or counseling.

General Learning Strategy

- Prefer to brainstorm questions and ideas, want an impression of the whole topic and freedom to explore their own questions.
- Learning strategies employed: active problem-solving discussions, imagining how to use a particular idea or observation, experimenting with objects.
- Learning enhanced by making linkages among ideas and personal values, visualizing the future, personal use of information or ideas.

Exemplary Development Comment

- "I usually address situations in private with other individuals without bringing undo attention to an issue or problem. Sometimes this takes too long and it fails. If my superiors want me to do something that is questionable, I remove myself from that decision, which limits my ability to influence the situation. I need to change this strategy."
- "I generate many ideas—often too many, because others get overwhelmed. People often don't know my priorities because I don't close the loop with them and then walk off thinking that all I said was important to do. Focus, direction, and limiting distractions are important for me to do to become more successful."

Extraverted Thinking

with Introverted Sensing

Basic Habits of Mind

As leaders, ESTJs give a critical, analytical eye to experience. They seek order and reasonableness in decision-making processes. Their dominant Extraverted Thinking works for a systematic task-focused action orientation. Aided with an auxiliary Introverted Sensing, ESTJs have clear impressions about experiences, people, and circumstances. This type enjoys methodical, systematic analysis of life events.

Typical Communication Patterns

- They are seen as giving high energy, tough minded expressions that are practical and realistic about situations before them.
- They like facts and are drawn to ask questions for clarity and precision.
- Their remarks are logical, orderly, and seem quite decisive.

Motivated and Motivates By

- The logical framework, the specific facts, and a systematic method to address a situation.
- A thorough critique that is orderly and practical moves them into action.

Observed Effective Behaviors

- They are seen as one of the highest rated types for doing what it takes, being decisive, confronting problems, and working the plan.
- Their demanding and deliberate style is often effective at leading others.

Insights Rarely Shared

- They think of themselves as resourceful, as a quick study, and a good team player.
- They view their straightforward style as an asset.

Blind Spots

- They may be surprised to learn that others feel that difficulties with interpersonal relationships are going to cause them problems.
- Observers feel they will have special difficulty when making strategic transitions.

Potential Barriers to Effectiveness

- They need to learn more effective ways to build and mend relationships.
- Of special concern, ESTJs need to focus on creating a developmental climate with direct reports or team members.

Extraverted Thinking

with Introverted Sensing

- Often technically competent, they mistake conformance to their instructions as respect for their ability.

Stress Related Behavior

- They may become more demanding and instructive as stressors are pressing on them.
- As stress increases, they are seen as aggressive, arrogant, and stingy with resources.
- With enough stress, they become hypersensitive to rejection and focus on the incompetence of those around them.

Entrepreneurial Mindset

- They like being in charge and make sure all of the procedures are followed.
- As a general rule, when they see strategic opportunities, they are effective at creating new organizations.
- They are attracted to the details of a range of industries, from computer programming to tool making.

General Learning Strategy

- Prefer sequential, active, competitive, problem-solving opportunities when learning new ideas or frameworks.
- Learning strategies employed: "doing something" with information, listing facts.
- Learning enhanced by demonstrations, practical activities, and hands-on learning.

Exemplary Development Comment

- "I have overdone the hard driving, high expectations, performance at any cost trait until it has hurt relationships, failed to put people at ease, and caused others to stop challenging me for making changes. These are not good outcomes for the company and not good for me."
- "In the past I've had the attitude that if I couldn't be a major influencer, then I didn't want to be part of the group. My 'take charge' perspective has clearly affected my ability to listen to others' point of view and to be over controlling. It is not that I achieve the wrong results. It is in the way I go about achieving results which has to change—be more patient, listen more, and trust others to do their part."

Extraverted Thinking

with Introverted Intuition

Basic Habits of Mind

ENTJs as leaders are inclined to critique and analyze information as it occurs in relation to some larger framework. Their dominant function, Extraverted Thinking, initiates questions like: *What are the assumptions, and conclusions, and are these reasonable?* Their Introverted Intuition serves to identify endless connections and interrelationships among facts and ideas. ENTJs are perpetually building more complex models of whatever their interests may be.

Typical Communication Patterns

- Expressive and fluent about their ideas and their critique of events or situations, the dominant extraverted thinking function leads to discussing theory, analyses, and a formula for making things work better.
- They are fast paced in their interactions, action oriented, and communicate high aspirations.

Motivated and Motivates By

- Systematic and logical action; looking for ways to improve whatever has gone before in anticipation of the future state of affairs.
- Ideas and global issues.
- Energized by making things happen and by the process of actualizing ideas.

Observed Effective Behaviors

- Seen as effectively decisive and acting to do whatever it takes to get the job done, they also appear to be effective when they are organized, deliberate, and assertive.
- Seen as responsible and forthright individuals, ENTJs are often effective in leading others when being sociable and inclusive.

Insights Rarely Shared

- They may not talk about it, but they see themselves as resourceful and effective at confronting others.
- They feel they are a quick study and know how to put people at ease.

Blind Spots

- Creating a developmental climate and building relationships.
- Their attention to task contributions for their team is far greater than their building and mending relationships in team work.

Extraverted Thinking

with Introverted Intuition

Potential Barriers to Effectiveness

- Observers feel that they could have problems with interpersonal relationships because of their quick verbal analytical style.
- Problems with personal/work balance are created by their high aspirations and demanding attitudes.
- Their general proactive attitudes and critical nature can be seen as condescending and arrogant.

Stress Related Behavior

- As stressors increase, ENTJs become aggressive and arrogant.
- With enough stress, they put more energy into "getting the job done and getting it done right!! Now!"
- After prolonged stress, they may seem detached, reserved, hypersensitive, and somewhat overly concerned about others' views and opinions of them.

Entrepreneurial Mindset

- Usually their ability to conceive and act on a business plan is so well developed that they are likely to be found in the startup of any number of industries such as business consulting, personnel and human resource services, and health-related administration.
- They are as invested in the theory of business and how to make various businesses work as they are in the particulars of a given business.

General Learning Strategy

- Prefer the big picture and a challenging assignment when learning.
- Learning strategies employed: debating ideas, independently researching.
- Learning enhanced by complex problems to solve and by providing an environment which rewards achievement and demonstrated analysis.

Exemplary Development Comment

- "I am so energetic in gathering data and asking questions that I alienate others which makes me look abrasive and less personable. I am so self-reliant, independent, and demanding that I do not take time to study, listen, and engage in more personal ways with others."
- "My analytical strengths lead to me over reacting and seeming less compassionate than I really am. I need to utilize more of a participative leader style more frequently."

Extraverted Feeling

with Introverted Sensing

Basic Habits of Mind

ESFJ leaders give a great deal of attention to people and their reactions to situations. Immediately aware of the relationships among people, their dominant function of Extraverted Feeling expressively seeks to understand others' experiences. Responsive, loyal, and attuned to others are qualities emerging from their dominant function. The auxiliary function of Introverted Sensing aids ESFJs by supplying immediate impressions of people and situations which are factual and detailed.

Typical Communication Patterns

- Upon meeting ESFJs, most people feel that these individuals are warm and outgoing.
- While they like to make decisions, get clarity, and make sure instructions are clear, they are also eager to communicate inclusion by being empathetic.
- They make unassuming observations and they like conversation that is focused on people-related topics.

Motivated and Motivates By

- Practical, realistic, hands-on action, which moves toward completion of a project or task.
- They enjoy the moment and are energized by their activities as long as these are guided by definitive guidelines and timelines.

Observed Effective Behaviors

- Their decisive, hands-on, do-what-it-takes style is seen as effective.
- They take a conventional approach to everyday work issues.
- They appear precise in their judgments and demanding in getting the job done.

Insights Rarely Shared

- ESFJs see themselves as resourceful, flexible, straightforward, and very able to create developmental climates at work.
- They believe that their teamwork skills enable them to build relationships and effectively aid the organization in achieving its goals.

Blind Spots

- Others believe that they may develop problems with interpersonal relationships if they fail to learn how to be more changeable and delegating.
- They appear to have problems when organizations are making strategic transitions and changes.

Extraverted Feeling

with Introverted Sensing

Potential Barriers to Effectiveness

- At times, their energy for closure and focus comes across as blunt, abrasive and manipulating.
- The appearance of being pressuring works against their effectiveness.
- Unless they demonstrate more innovativeness and openness to change, ESFJs may not identify key opportunities for growth and development.

Stress Related Behavior

- As they experience stress, ESFJs appear more energetic and insist on cooperation from others. This leads to hasty observations and unrealistic expectations.
- Under prolonged stress, they will resort to being quite guarded and when they do engage, they become overly nit picking.
- They seem unusually unemotional, overly conventional and obsessive about the current situation they are in.

Entrepreneurial Mindset

- Given the opportunity to start up their own operation, they may choose help-related businesses. Expect to see them develop home management consulting, health support services, food services, or mechanical and technical related companies.
- They like to provide pragmatic services that have a high person contact and high product output component, such as a local copier service.

General Learning Strategy

- Prefer to learn in a cooperative environment with active personal sharing.
- Learning strategies employed: actively networking with others to share ideas, creating a systematic structure to understand information.
- Learning enhanced by exploring practical use of information and experience, demonstrating the personal value and worthwhile nature of information.

Exemplary Development Comment

- "I tend to make sure my feelings favor a certain situation. I need to give myself a reason for involvement so I will do my best job. While my concern for others makes people comfortable, the energy level sometimes intimidates. I need to slow down, be more open to others' ideas, and give others time to share their ideas—give people airtime."

Extraverted Feeling

with Introverted Intuition

Basic Habits of Mind

ENFJ leaders are expressive, positive, and look for structured ways to achieve the goal and maintain relationships. Their dominant Extraverted Feeling connects with people in intense ways and is often in tune with the subtle differences of interpersonal interactions among people. They are very engaging and affiliative. This interest in people is aided by Introverted Intuition which triggers their imagining of a variety of possibilities for each person with whom they are engaged, and innovative and imaginative solutions to problems they confront.

Typical Communication Patterns

- They like to create conversations that lead to cooperation, to the sharing of ideas, and to exploring new possibilities.
- They are expressive and gregarious, covering a variety of topics in any conversation.
- Being appreciative and supportive of others are common expressions they put forth.

Motivated and Motivates By

- Working with people issues rather than technical.
- Being resourceful about human behaviors and possibilities, they get excited by affiliative interactions that enable them to share the patterns and insights they feel are important.
- Energizing with their initiating and approachable nature.

Observed Effective Behaviors

- Highly rated for leading others with enthusiasm and warmth, they are seen as able communicators who put people at ease and get the job done.
- Perceived as good at developing relationships and being appropriately compassionate, they are seen as effective due to their energetic, initiating, methodical, and forceful style.

Insights Rarely Shared

- They feel they have a strong sense of appropriate decisive action and work well on teams.
- They feel that they have a good balance of work and personal life that serves them in leading others.

Blind Spots

- They would be surprised to hear that others think they need to be more flexible and less critical of upper management.
- Many feel they have an overdependence on a select few.

Extraverted Feeling

with Introverted Intuition

Potential Barriers to Effectiveness

- They need to address their behaviors that appear more opinionated, manipulating, blunt, and dogmatic.
- At times their energetic style seems pressuring, their methodical approach seems manipulating, and their comments seem overly personal.

Stress Related Behavior

- When under stress, ENFJs put more energy into being decisive—and thus seem pushy—and taking action, which seems impatient.
- As this increases, they seem hasty, impulsive, and hardheaded.
- With sustained stress, they become reserved, retiring, and obsessed with internal criticisms of their perceived failures and inadequate accomplishments.

Entrepreneurial Mindset

- They have a clear vision of the business and how to utilize people to actualize that vision. They are involved with crisis support services, general consulting, and spiritual support activities and endeavors.
- Irrespective of their choice of career and industry, they have an uncanny capacity to read the marketplace, although usually they concern themselves with businesses that have a capacity to change and evolve.

General Learning Strategy

- Prefer to learn by creative exploration and like to discover connections among ideas and people.
- Learning strategies employed: networking with others to explore connections and future uses of information, quickly envisioning how experience is valuable.
- Learning enhanced by opportunities to share insights, explore speculations, and experience a supportive environment to test out ideas and creative expressions.

Exemplary Development Comment

- "I tend to begin working on solving the problem before completely analyzing it! I overlook some opportunities for learning because I focus too much on other people."
- "I probably consult too much with others, leading to more time in relationship building than in fact assessment or selling my own ideas. I am very innovative but not do persuasively share my vision when I facilitate group problem-solving."

Making the Most of This Guide as a Leader

Knowing oneself well and understanding how others may differ are fundamental ingredients to strong relationships and effective leadership. In this guide we show how these factors—self-knowledge, relationship building and leadership—are related and support each other. The key facts about leadership and these factors are:

- First, leadership is about behavior. Behavior, especially as related to communication, gives strong clues as to our leadership style.

- Second, to enhance effectiveness, leaders need to fully understand the patterns in their current behavior and to *recognize* and *employ* the range of behaviors available to them.

- Third, a psychology of leadership as suggested by psychological type invites individuals to recognize their demonstrated behaviors as expressions of their type, and to see type development as a way to enhance overall leader development. Through type development, we become clear about our habits of mind, and about when our other preferences (behavior potentials) should be used.

Stretching beyond our typical habits may require a change in awareness and in expressed behavior. Most of us are willing to consider making changes in our behavior when we feel the need. Sometimes the need is imposed on us. People have given us feedback that we need to adjust "or else." Sometimes we change because of an internal awareness that to reach higher levels of satisfaction and pleasure in our endeavors, we must stretch our comfort zones.

But change is often difficult. Our current behaviors have been developed over years of hard work and we do not give them up easily. Usually, our behaviors have lots of support in one way or another—like the comfortable feeling we get from "knowing what to do." More often than not, we have moved down a path in life that has reinforced some of our basic assumptions about the future and about who we are. In an environment of dynamic change, we come to realize that many of these assumptions no longer serve us well as leaders.

When we take up the challenge of personal change, it means we are eager to discover new things, try out new ideas and behaviors, and are open to experiences we have not fully understood. In a similar fashion, this guide suggests some of the dynamics underlying our current behaviors, how others have observed and rated them, and ways to stretch to some new possibilities.

Learn from the Insights

Use this guide to learn about the various expressions of your type and how others observe these. Identify those qualities that increase your energy and consider those things you feel about yourself but do not necessarily share with others.

Step One—Clarify Data

So you can recognize the *full range* of behaviors which you use, go through the guide and read all sixteen leadership type descriptions. Earlier in this guide you were asked to *underline* all those behaviors which you know you demonstrate from each of the types and to *[bracket]* those behaviors from each of the types you know you should demonstrate more often to enhance your effectiveness. Using the information generated by this exploration of the types, complete the following framework below for your personal analysis and developmental planning.

In much the same way as the Johari Window[10] model opens our understanding of information in an interaction, we have the opportunity to peer at ourselves from the descriptions in this guide through the panes of:

- Observed Effectiveness (what I know and they know);
- Insights Rarely Shared (what I know and they don't know about me);
- Blind Spots and Barriers (what they know about me that I may not know).

Such self-observation can lead to valuable insights about the *consequences of our behavior on those around us and the importance of making conscious choices about how we behave.*

Below is a suggested format for "working through" this information to enhance your developmental planning. From the analysis provided in the description of your type and your identification of strengths and undemonstrated behaviors from the other fifteen descriptions, identify three key leadership growth priorities. Repeat the recommended format for each of the top three leadership development priorities you have which need deeper exploration. For example, if a top priority for you is to increase the range of communication skills you have, then looking at the typical communication patterns of your type and developing a comparison with the other types is likely to be very fruitful.

Making the Most of This Guide as a Leader

Leadership Development Priority (Identify a Specific Dimension)

Look at the leadership behavior clusters listed on pages seven and eight of this guide and in Appendix A. Consider how your various type related behaviors affect relationship building, communication, decisiveness, etc.

Those behaviors which I know are true of me in this dimension	The potential unintended negative messages or consequences from these behaviors
Those behaviors which I know I need to express to become more effective in this dimension	The potentially positive outcomes from increasing the frequency of these behaviors

Step Two—Create Hypotheses

Review some of your analyses and hypotheses about your type and your behavior with individuals who can become learning partners. Identify for them the relationship between your expressed preferences and feedback you have received. Through questions and examples, identify the patterns and themes in your behavior that you see as valuable to explore.

Step Three—Set Goals

Following this analysis, you need to set three goals to enhance your effectiveness. For each goal:

- write a simple, descriptive, measurable, and specific goal;
- be sure to identify what must change to make the goal achievable and the supports needed to maintain the goal in the long term.

As an example, consider: "When in meetings, I will make a specific point of asking each member of the team for their opinions and ideas. Far too often I have provided plans and given directions without their participation. I will ask for co-chairs to give me feedback about soliciting others' views. I believe this new behavior will increase buy-in and motivation toward the tasks ahead."

Development Goal *(Specific, Measurable, Achievable)*

Adjustments to make the goal achievable

Support needed to make the goal sustainable

Enhancements to effectiveness if goal is achieved

If you create reasonable, practical goals for your development, you will see enhancements in your style in the months ahead. Recognizing that you have the potential to express a range of behaviors and practicing these less frequent behaviors is important to your development as a leader. But you should remember that this is a work in progress. For example, if you are particularly good at making logical arguments and you are working on being more demonstrative in your appreciation of others, you will need many tries and much feedback about your efforts.

To further your developmental goals:

- Do ask others from work, home, and other social groups what they see as your most effective qualities.
- Do ask others what you could do to improve your effectiveness.
- Do seek out ways to get ongoing feedback.
- Do collect facts, identify patterns, focus on how you get particular outcomes, and examine the congruence of your values and behaviors.

For the Leader Coach

Coaching a leader is an important role that can be enhanced with the use of psychological type. Leader coaches are concerned with the leader's development of crucial competencies for organizational success. These competencies include communicating, problem-solving, learning effectiveness, monitoring self-awareness, and clarifying professional goals and directions. Often the leader coach has to focus on leader style, management of change, and leader personality as a way to highlight the needed competencies in today's dynamic organizations. Psychological type, because of its unique focus on the way an individual processes and adapts to the world, covers the bases for leaders' learning and development.

In the broadest sense, leader coaches want to cover both leader abilities and goals, and organizational perceptions and standards of and for the leader. While the psychological type of a leader does not inform us about abilities and capacities to achieve various standards, it does help us clarify how an individual is likely to approach learning and implement what is learned to enhance competencies, and how a leader may be perceived. Psychological type invites us to consider the development of the individual and the role of the interplay between the public (extraverted world) and the private (introverted) world of the leader.

If you are a leader coach and using this guide, there are several important points to keep in mind. Integrating the material in this guide with other data on the manager or executive will result in the greatest value for your client. Consider these stages of use as a coach:

Stage 1—*Identify all uses of the type preferences and functions.*

This affirms both the use and the capacity to use these functions.

- When reviewing type, ask the client to identify a *specific business example* of how they use Extraversion, Introversion, Sensing, Intuition, Thinking, and Feeling.
- As you introduce type dynamics, ask for examples which illustrate Extraverted and Introverted Sensing, Extraverted and Introverted Intuition, Extraverted and Introverted Thinking, Extraverted and Introverted Feeling. Some prompters are provided in Appendix A of this booklet.

Stage 2—*Focus on their particular type and link with the data you have.*

This shows the practical outcomes of their habits of mind.

- Using their examples, this guide, and other data collected on their behavior, you can enable the leader to see the nature of their mental habits, how these play out and affect others, and

For the Leader Coach

how they can become more intentional about expressing those areas of their typology (about which they have given examples) in appropriate ways.

Stage 3—*Move into developmental planning to encourage recognition and employment of their type potentials—those preferences outside of their habits of mind. The steps in this stage are outlined below.*

Using the data presented in this booklet and material provided during the coaching session, consider working through the following steps to make the most of the type related material.

Step 1: List the important type related issues in the grid below.

Self-Assessed Type Related Strengths	*Type Related Developmental Areas*
Type Related Perceptions by Key Organizational Members	*Type Related Expressions Others Feel are Needed for Effectiveness*

This gives you and your client a chance to explore personal strengths and organizational needs, and personal goals and organizational perceptions. Gaps clearly need to be explored.

Step 2: *Explore the personal motivation and the level of organizational support the leader is going to receive to make developmental changes. Use the format below to explore this area.*

Step 3: *Effectiveness Goal (as suggested by Step 1).*

Support for this goal comes from _____

Strategies to employ to monitor performance of this goal _____

_____

Benefits of achieving this goal are _____

Step 4: *Develop a follow-up plan with the leader. When, how, what and where will there be follow-up for checking on the implementation of this goal.*

Follow up date _____ How _____

Remember that when the leader learns to demonstrate a range of behaviors as suggested by type, the leader will be more effective. But for this to work the leader must want to enhance his or her range of behavior and the support must be present in the organization for the changes to really work.

Good coaching to you and good type development to your leader!

Appendix A

Type Expressions
and Leader Behavior

As suggested earlier, our type processes or capacities are easily identified in leader behavior. Keep in mind that the following list illustrates the *expression* of these mental capacities. This does not mean that only those with these preferences demonstrate the behavior; rather, it means that the behavior is an expression of a capacity we all have and should learn to appropriately express, as the situation requires. The type capacities listed merely reflect a primary and initial type process used in expressing the behavior. This list is the by-product of many leaders and managers identifying various skills according to their types.

While all type preferences must be used to some degree to execute the competencies listed below, a few of the preferences are proposed as primary for each cluster.

Relationship of Type Preferences and Leader Behaviors

Administrative Behaviors
(Using processes to analyze, prioritize, and document plans)

Competency Category	Related Type Preference Used
• *Establish plans*	T_I, S_I
• *Structure and policies*	T_I, S_I
• *Develop systems and processes*	T_I, N_I
• *Manage implementation of projects*	T_I, S_I, T_E
• *Work efficiency*	T_I, S_I, S_E

Communication Behaviors
(Knowing when to share or extravert information and being very intentional by thinking through or introverting about what is said as a manager and leader)

Competency Category	Related Type Preference Used
• *Speaking effectively*	N_E, T_E, F_E
• *Fostering open communication*	N_E, F_E
• *Listening to others*	F_I, S_E, S_I, F_E
• *Informing appropriately*	S_E, T_E
• *Delivering presentations*	N_E, T_E
• *Preparing written communication*	S_I, T_I
• *Confronting effectively*	F_E

Appendix A

Type Expressions
and Leader Behavior

Interpersonal Behaviors
(Showing interest in others and seeking to promote their well-being, demonstrating compassion and sensitivity to others)

Competency Category	Related Type Preference Used
• Building relationships	F_E
• Approachability	F_E
• Displaying organizational savvy	N_E
• Leveraging networks	N_E, T_E
• Valuing diversity	N_E, F_E
• Managing disagreements	T_E
• Demonstrating compassion	F_E
• Exhibiting good humor.	N_E, S_E
• Managing boss relationships	T_E
• Exhibiting patience	F_I, T_I

Executive Behaviors
(Demonstrating control, structure, direction, and order while coaching others and actively managing change issues)

Competency Category	Related Type Preference Used
• Providing direction	T_E
• Exhibiting courage	N_E, T_E
• Influencing others	N_E, S_E
• Fostering teamwork	F_E
• Motivating others	N_E, F_E
• Coaching and developing others	T_E, F_E
• Championing change	N_E
• Delegating effectively	T_E
• Planning and setting priorities	T_I
• Managing through systems	N_I, T_I

Appendix A

Motivation Behaviors
(Demonstrating an interest in others, providing support and challenge, and showing an openness to future possibilities)

Competency Category	Related Type Preference Used
• Drive for results	T_E
• Show work commitments	T_E
• Action oriented	T_E, N_E
• Perseverance	S_E, T_E
• Learning oriented	N_E, S_E
• Demonstrating commitments for developing others	N_E, F_E

Organizational Strategy Behaviors
(Demonstrating attention to tactical and visionary activities, some evidence of linking systems and market forces)

Competency Category	Related Type Preference Used
• Manage profitability	S_E, T_E, S_I
• Commit to quality	S_E, T_E
• Focus on customer needs	N_E, F_E
• Promote corporate citizenship	F_E
• Recognize global implications	N_E
• Innovation management	N_I, T_E

Self-Management Behavior
(Knowing oneself and exhibiting efforts to learn and grow)

Competency Category	Related Type Preference Used
• Acting with integrity	ALL TYPES
• Demonstrating adaptability	N_E
• Developing oneself	ALL TYPES
• Composure	T_E
• Intellectual horsepower	ALL TYPES

Appendix A

Thinking Skills

(Reasonable and rational behavior is highly prized in organizational life. We often get clarity in our assumptions and premises and analyze our choices accordingly.)

Competency Category	Related Type Preference Used
• *Think strategically*	N_E, T_E, T_I
• *Critically analyzing issues*	T_E
• *Demonstrating sound judgment*	T_I, T_E
• *Innovating*	N_E
• *Dealing with ambiguity*	N_E, S_E

Appendix B

Psychological Type
Framework Revisited

While the introduction to this guide provides a cursory look at type dimensions, you might explore the model further by considering an analogy. When we are learning a skill, we do not simply jump into a new area with high level proficiency. If we decided to take a training program in Karate, we would start with learning basic concepts like simple movement (such as tumbling) and then move to complex activities (such as using opponents' movement in our favor). Once this level of skill is accomplished, we move to integrating movement and action into Karate strategies for defense and offense. We begin with gaining clarity about the basics before we transform information into more dynamic and complex material. The same is true with psychological type. We need first to get clarity about the basic concepts such as extraverting, introverting, etc., and then move to the psychological complexity of type dynamics.

Basic Assumptions of Type

Type assumes that:

- Each individual utilizes all of the processes of type in varying degrees and with different levels of awareness of use.
- Each individual balances psychological energy through extraverting and introverting processes.
- Each individual needs to take in information (a perceptive process) and to make decisions about it (a judgment process).
- Each individual has habits of mind in the use of extraverting and introverting processes which happen with such consistency as to give us a psychological typology.

In the simplest form, the following qualities are associated with each dimension of psychological type. The purpose of the following list is to prepare us to identify our preferences.

Extraversion
- *Initiating, expressive, active*
- *Talks about thoughts, feelings*
- *Likes knowing via experience*

Introversion
- *Careful about engaging, quiet, appears reflective*
- *Succinct*
- *Likes written material and knowing by thinking inside*

Sensing
- *Focuses on tangible, concrete*
- *Deliberate, practical*
- *Enjoys known activities*

Intuition
- *See new "ideas," patterns*
- *Imaginative, abstract*
- *Enjoys complexity*

Thinking
- *Prefers rational models*
- *Critically questions, seeks truth*
- *Thorough debate confirms decisions*

Feeling
- *Prefers ideals, values*
- *Seeks acceptance, agreeableness, tolerance*
- *Interdependence validates import of personal connections*

Appendix B

The MBTI enables you to sort on these three dimensions and the following fourth aspect of type. Isabel Myers' addition of the *Judgment and Perception* dimension serves the purpose of enabling us to identify type dynamics. Very specifically, Myers wanted to identify the mental process *used in the external, extraverted world for all types*. She reasoned that since all types extravert a mental function (either what we perceive or judge), she created the JP scale for that purpose. It assumes that the mental function **not** used in the outer, extraverted world is used in the inner, introverted world. This scale of the MBTI identifies use of a given mental function in the outer world and has the following characteristics:

Judging	Perceiving
• *Prefers closure, decision*	• *Prefers openness, waits for the "right time" to decide*
• *Organizes, uses systemic method*	• *Spontaneity, likes emerging awareness best*
• *Clarifies method, then acts*	• *Clarifies information and its importance, then acts*
• *Uses Thinking or Feeling in the outer world*	• *Uses Sensing or Intuition in the outer world*

Using the quick checklist above of the eight dimensions, and other supporting documents (such as ***Looking at Type*** ™ or ***Introduction to Type***®), list your four letter type code. Take the code and find the description in the central part of this booklet and read your description. If this does not "fit" for you, read the first few paragraphs of types with similar codes to identify the mental habit of mind, or type, that works for you.

Type Preference and Code Summary *(You are the expert, sort yourself)*

E or I____ S or N____ T or F____ J or P____ Code____ ____ ____ ____

Quick Check on Dynamics

As a reminder: one mental function like sensing or intuition, or thinking or feeling, is used in the external world and *the other* in the private, unseen, internal world. For example, an ENTJ and ISFJ both use extraverted judgment (thinking or feeling) and introverted perceiving (intuition or sensing). One of the key differences in these two types is tied to which type function is primary and which is secondary, which is thoroughly identified in the text of this booklet. As a short hand, the following table gives the dominant and auxiliary type process for each type.

Appendix B

Psychological Type Framework Revisited

The purpose of the table below is to quickly identify the extraverted-introverted dynamic for each of the sixteen types.

Keep in mind that the dynamic is the automatic pilot maintaining the balance between the psychological world outside and inside our skins. Think of it as an energy exchange system, moving in alternating currents.

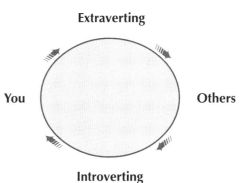

Type Code	Dominant	Auxiliary
ISTJ — *Introverted Sensing w/ Extraverted Thinking*	S_I	T_E
ISFJ — *Introverted Sensing w/ Extraverted Feeling*	S_I	F_E
INFJ — *Introverted Intuition w/ Extraverted Feeling*	N_I	F_E
INTJ — *Introverted Intuition w/ Extraverted Thinking*	N_I	T_E
ISTP — *Introverted Thinking w/ Extraverted Sensing*	T_I	S_E
ISFP — *Introverted Feeling w/ Extraverted Sensing*	F_I	S_E
INFP— *Introverted Feeling w/ Extraverted Intuition*	F_I	N_E
INTP— *Introverted Thinking w/ Extraverted Intuition*	T_I	N_E
ESTP — *Extraverted Sensing w/Introverted Thinking*	S_E	T_I
ESFP — *Extraverted Sensing w/Introverted Feeling*	S_E	F_I
ENFP— *Extraverted Intuition w/Introverted Feeling*	N_E	F_I
ENTP— *Extraverted Intuition w/Introverted Thinking*	N_E	T_I
ESTJ — *Extraverted Thinking w/Introverted Sensing*	T_E	S_I
ESFJ — *Extraverted Feeling w/Introverted Sensing*	F_E	S_I
ENFJ — *Extraverted Feeling w/Introverted Intuition*	F_E	N_I
ENTJ — *Extraverted Thinking w/Introverted Intuition*	T_E	N_I

Final reminder: Jung and Myers assumed that we used all of the mental functions (S, N, T, and F) in the various attitudes (E, I). So an interpretation that is appropriate to type looks at *preference and attitude* rather than simply dimensions of the type. In other words, an individual might have a preference for Extraverted Thinking and she also uses Introverted Thinking. She simply may not use it with the same level of awareness or pleasure.

References and Endnotes

To learn more about these dynamics, recheck the descriptions in this booklet and read some more extensive items on type as suggested below.

For additional explorations into leadership and type, you are encouraged to explore:

Hard Wired Leadership (1998) Roger R. Pearman, Davies-Black Publisher, Palo Alto, Ca.

I'm Not Crazy, I'm Just Not You (1997) Roger R. Pearman and Sarah Albritton, Davies-Black Publisher, Palo Alto, CA.

Developing Leaders: Research and Applications in Psychological Type and Leadership Development (1997) Catherine Fitzgerald and Linda Kirby, Davies-Black Publisher, Palo Alto, CA.

Leadership Development (1994) Norma Barr and Lee Barr, Eakin Press, Austin, TX.

Type Talk (1988) Otto Kroeger and Janet M. Thuesen, Delacorte Press, New York, NY.

To explore developmental issues of psychological type, consider:

Beside Ourselves (1997) Naomi Quenk, Davies-Black Publisher, Palo Alto, CA.

LifeKeys (1996) Kise, Stark, and Hirsh, Bethany House Publishers, Minneapolis, MN.

Navigating Midlife (1993) Eleanor Corlett and Nancy Millner, Davies-Black Publisher, Palo Alto, CA.

Endnotes

[1] In addition to the standard journals from which competency lists were made for this material, special note is given to numerous research studies at the Center for Creative Leadership, Greensboro, N.C. For an excellent review of the skills (from undeveloped to overused) essential to success, see *For Your Improvement* (1996) Lombardo, M. and Eichinger, R., Lominger Limited, Inc., Greensboro, N.C. Also see the *Successful Manager's Handbook*, Davis, B. et al, (1996) Personnel Decisions, PDI, USA.

[2] Martineau, J. and Van Velsor, E. (1997) The MBTI, Goals, and Change as a Result of a Leadership Development Program, *Proceedings of the Second International Research Conference on Leadership and the Myers-Briggs Type Indicator*, pp. 123-134.

[3] The model as presented by Carl G. Jung's *Psychological Types* (1921), Bolligen Press, Princeton, and Isabel B. Myers' *Gifts Differing* (1981), Palo Alto, CA: Consulting Psychologists Press.

[4] Pearman, R. (1992) *The Dynamic Energy of Type*, **Bulletin of Psychological Type**, 15, 4, pp.2-4; Pearman R. and Albrittion, S. (1997) *I'm Not Crazy, I'm Just Not You*. Palo Alto, CA: Davies-Black, p.10.

References and Endnotes

[5] Pearman, R. and Fleenor, J. (1996) *Differences in Observed and Self-Reported Qualities of Psychological Types*, **Journal of Psychological Type**, 39, pp. 3-16; Pearman, R. and Fleenor, J. (1997) *Sixteen Patterns of Leadership Effectiveness: A Multivariate Analysis of Observational Variables and the MBTI*, **Proceedings of the Second International Research Conference on Leadership and the Myers-Briggs Type Indicator**, pp. 183-212.

[6] Use has been made of the database at the Center for Creative Leadership. The Center is a not-for-profit educational executive training center with facilities in San Diego, Colorado Springs, Brussels, and headquarters in Greensboro, North Carolina. One of the largest providers of executive and manager training in the world, the CCL is dedicated to promoting research into managerial behavior. Through the support of the CCL, very sophisticated and detailed statistical analysis of their data has aided in the author's research. Specific instruments which are of special note are the *Effective Leadership Index and Benchmarks* which are published by the CCL. Benchmarks® is a registered trademark of the Center for Creative Leadership. For information on the Center for Creative Leadership, call 336-288-7210 or write Post Office Box 26300, Greensboro, North Carolina 27438-6300.

[7] *See I'm Not Crazy, I'm Just Not You* (1997), Palo Alto, CA: Davies-Black Publishing, Inc., by Roger R. Pearman and Sarah C. Albritton. This book reviews in more detail material gathered from over twenty years of work with the Myers-Briggs Type Indicator. The MBTI is not reviewed extensively in this guide to type effectiveness as there are many good sources of material available to review this instrument. Millions of individuals have taken the Indicator and are familiar with its concepts. For shorthand purposes, the reader may consider the review in the Appendix B of this guide.

[8] Hammer, A., Editor, (1997) *MBTI Applications: A Decade of Research*. Consulting Psychologists Press, Inc., p. 62; Maybee, R. *Effects of Psychological Type and Self-Perceived Power on Situational Leadership Style Adaptability*, paper presented at the CAPT Conference on Leadership and the MBTI, April 2-4, 1997, Washington, D.C.

[9] Material initially published by Roger R. Pearman in 1983 for a presentation at a meeting of the Association for Psychological Type. Reissued with updates in 1987, 1989, 1993, 1995 as *Introduction to the Teacher Within: Explorations of the Inferior Functions* by Roger Pearman and Sarah Albritton (editor), Leadership Innovations, Winston-Salem, NC. The material was incorporated as Chapter 4, *The Teacher Within*, in ***I'm Not Crazy, I'm Just Not You: The Real Meaning of the Sixteen Personality Types***, Palo Alto, CA: Davies-Black Publisher, Inc.

[10] The Johari Window was developed by Joseph Luft and Harry Ingham over two decades ago to illustrate the importance of feedback. Their simple model was that during interactions there were four panes in the window: things the observer and person know, things the person knows but the observer does not, things the observer knows but does not share with the person, and things that neither know but are present in the interaction. See Hanson, P.G. (1973) The johari window: A model for soliciting and giving feedback. In J.W. Pfeiffer & J.E. Jones (Eds.), *The 1973 annual handbook for group facilitators*. San Diego, CA: University Associates.